Inside the Mind of...

Susan Greenfield – Brain Scientist

written by Pam Bishop
illustrated by Jeff Anderson, Kathy Baxendale
and Chris Brown

Contents

At school in the 1950s	2
My proudest moments	4
My childhood and family	6
Teenage years	8
Going to university	10
My first interest in the brain	12
Starting research work	14
Alzheimer's and Parkinson's diseases	16
What makes me do my work?	18
Who I really am	20
Working at the Royal Institution	22
A typical day in Oxford	24
A typical week in my life	26
What have we learned about the brain?	28
What might we learn in the future?	30
Index	32

At school in the 1950s

At my nursery school

Do you like the bow in my hair?

Painting is very serious work

1950
Born in Chiswick, West London

1953
Started nursery at Beverly Infant School

1957
Went to Cavendish Primary School

With my best friend

and our hamsters

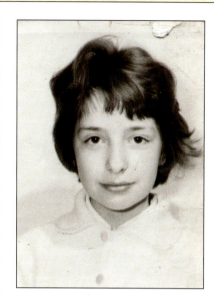

Growing up and nearly ready to go to secondary school

Can't wait to start at my new school

With my mum and friend Patsy – keeping cool!

1962
Started secondary school at Godolphin and Latymer School for Girls

1968
Did A level examinations

My proudest moments

A proud day when I got my degree at Oxford

Shahin and I have been friends since we were four years old

At Buckingham Palace, receiving my **CBE**

1969	**1970**	**1973**	**1977**	**1979**
Spent a year living on a **kibbutz** in Israel	Started at St Hilda's College in Oxford University	Became Susan Greenfield BA (Hons) Oxon	Became Dr Susan Greenfield	Working as a research neuroscientist in Paris

With Mum and one of my old teachers with my new book

Now I'm an author as well as a scientist!

At the Royal Institution where I work now

Glossary

CBE: Commander of the Order of the British Empire, an honour given by the Queen or King

Kibbutz: a community farm in Israel

1985	1996	1997	1998	2000	2001
Appointed as a university lecturer in Oxford	Became Professor of Pharmacology in Oxford	Set up Synaptica	Became Director of the Royal Institution of Great Britain	Went to Buckingham Palace to receive the CBE	Entered the House of Lords as Baroness Greenfield

My childhood and family

For thirteen years I was an only child and until my brother was born I was my parents' 'little star'. I am sure that my mum and dad gave me the confidence to do all that I have been able to achieve in my life. But they never let me get too big for my boots.

My mother Doris was a dancer on the stage before she married. After that she looked after the house and family. I went to ballet classes with my friends and, like my mum, I enjoyed dressing up and performing for an audience.

My mum, when she was a dancer

Reg, my dad, loves machines. He can fix anything and he liked repairing our old car and getting it ready for family trips out at the weekend. We used to take picnics into the countryside and to places like Heathrow airport to watch the planes. We went on holiday every summer to the seaside at Brighton or Eastbourne but we never went abroad. I never imagined that one day I would be flying to exotic countries all over the world!

Mum and Dad did not have the chance to stay on at school but they always tried to help me with my homework. Mum says that I started to read when I was about three years old and I have always been a bookworm. Even when I was young I used to go to the adult library to get out books on history or **geology** or **politics**.

My dad was always fixing something

Glossary

geology: study of the structure of the earth
politics: study of how government works

Teenage years

When I left my primary school I passed an exam so that I could go to a large secondary school for girls. I used to walk there with a friend. I loved it and enjoyed all the new and different subjects we did there. My favourite teacher was Miss Veronica Lemon who taught Greek. She was young and lively and although she made us work very hard, it was great fun.

Sadly, I did not really enjoy science at school because in those days it did not make me think about interesting ideas. I am sure it must be better now. I believe that all young people should study science so that they can understand more about their bodies and the world around them.

As a teenager I was mad about horses. I used to read books about ponies, dreaming that one day I would have one of my own. I never did, but I worked in a local shop on Saturdays so that I could earn enough money to pay for riding lessons on Wimbledon Common.

It was about this time that my brother Graham was born. I thought he was a real nuisance. I can remember that my mum got very tired having to get up to feed him in the middle of the night and do all the extra washing. He used to annoy me by bumping into me with his baby walker. One day I did something very mischievous just to torment him. I put his plastic water pistol in the oven and melted it!

We get on fine now that we are grown up but I have never wanted to have children of my own – there have always seemed to be too many books to read and interesting things to do.

I stayed at school until I was eighteen and did A levels in Ancient History, Maths, Latin and Greek. I was fascinated by how people lived thousands of years ago and the ideas that they had about life.

I still have this interest in big ideas about people and the world. My parents did not have very much money but I did well in my exams and I was fortunate to be awarded a special prize so that I could go to study PPP (**Philosophy**, Politics and **Psychology**) at Oxford University. It seemed far from my home and a very different world from the one that I was used to in our small London flat.

A painting of Oxford from 1793. Some of the buildings are still there today.

Glossary

philosophy: the study of ideas and beliefs
psychology: the study of the mind and behaviour

Going to university

I went to St Hilda's College in Oxford.

Life in St Hilda's College in Oxford turned out to be wonderful. I made lots of friends and we used to drink coffee together, listening to music and talking for hours. I especially liked the beautiful old buildings, the walks in the parks and the college gardens. One of the most exciting things is to go punting on the river, which means that you push the boat along with a long pole. There are excellent bookshops in the city and I liked meeting so many different sorts of people. We had to dress up in black gowns for dinner and we had things to eat that I had never had at home. There were always parties to go to. But of course we had to work hard too!

Punting down the river in Oxford

I became fascinated by how people think and what makes them behave in certain ways. For example:

- What makes us happy or sad?
- Why are we interested in some things at school but not others?
- Why do some people like working in teams but others prefer to do things on their own?

I was so interested in these sorts of questions that I changed my university course to study only Psychology. Psychology is the science of how we think and behave. It was the start of my interest in the brain, and work that I will do for the rest of my life. Since I had not done very much science at school it was a big change for me, but I loved my new studies and I knew that I had made the right decision.

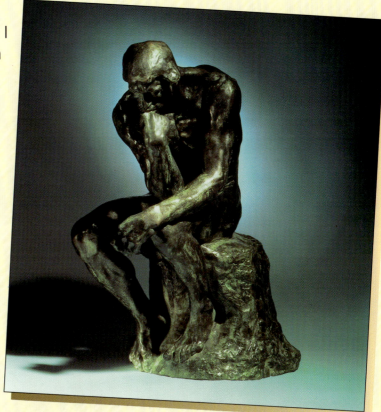

This sculpture is called 'The Thinker' and was made by Auguste Rodin. It can be found in the Rodin museum in Paris.

My first interest in the brain

It was one day in the laboratory, during my first year at university, that I knew I wanted to find out more about the brain. There in a dish on the bench was this creamy coloured, wrinkled, soft lump of material no bigger than the palm of my hand and weighing just over one kilogram. Yet I knew that it did such wonderful things.

Are you ready to get your brain working? Because I am going to tell you some things about it!

The human brain is the most complicated piece of machinery that we know. It is much more complicated and clever than the most expensive computer.

The largest part of the brain is the *cerebrum*. It is made up of two halves called the *cerebral hemispheres* and it looks a bit like a cauliflower!

The *cerebellum*, or 'little brain', controls our balance and co-ordination when we walk or ride a bike.

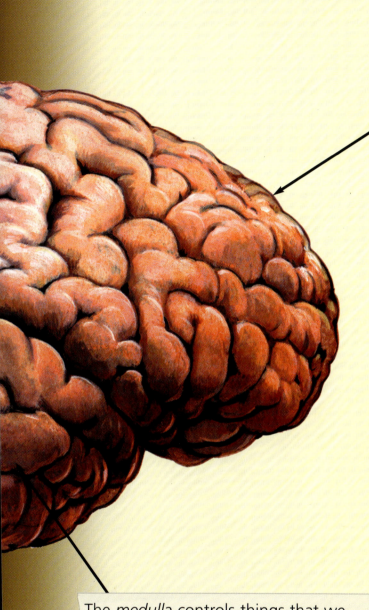

The *cortex* is the outer layer of the cerebrum. It is only one millimetre thick and is made of "grey matter". It is very important for

- receiving messages coming into the brain from sense organs such as the eyes, ears, nose, tongue and skin. We know what is happening in the world outside.

- sending messages out of the brain to muscles all over the body, e.g. in our arms and legs. We can move and take action.

- making connections between messages coming into the brain and information we have remembered from before. We can make conscious decisions about the actions we take.

The *medulla* controls things that we take for granted like how fast our heart is beating and how the temperature of our body stays steady.

Starting research work

After three years as a student in Oxford I was Susan Greenfield BA (Hons), which meant I had an Honours degree in Psychology. But I wanted to stay on to do research and find out even more about the brain. I was about to become a **neuroscientist**.

Life as a young research scientist is hard. There is so much to learn and so much to do. Progress is very slow and you are never sure if you are doing the right thing. However I was determined to enjoy it all so I did not take myself too seriously.

I did experiments in the laboratory, read lots of books in the famous Oxford libraries and talked to older and more experienced scientists. They helped me to understand the things that I was discovering. My main interest was in a chemical called *acetylcholinesterase*. This probably does several jobs in the brain but I was sure that if I could find out more about it, we might be able to help people with brain diseases.

In 1977 I successfully finished my first project and became Dr Susan Greenfield. My parents were very proud of me but I knew that this was only the beginning of a life's work.

The Bodleian library in Oxford is one of my favourite places to do research

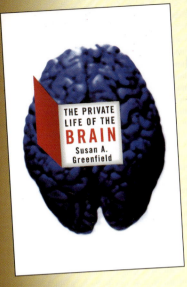

For the next ten years I continued to research and study the brain but now I worked in Paris, in the USA and in other parts of the world. In 1985 I went back to Oxford to be a university lecturer and in 1996 I was promoted to be a Professor there. This is like being the head teacher of a school. I had students to teach, laboratory work to do, paperwork to sort out and other staff to look after. This is one of the main jobs that I still do today.

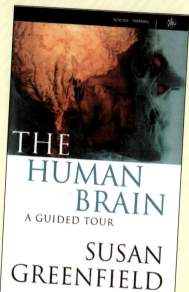

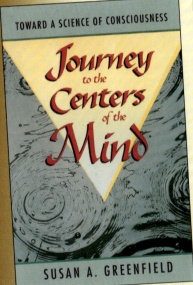

I had found out so many interesting and new things about the brain that I also started to write books about it. I dedicated one of my books to my mum and dad who, like many older people, had not done much science at school. I think it is important that everybody knows as much as possible about the brain.

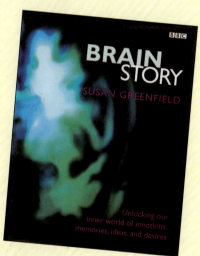

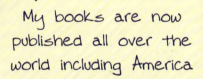

My books are now published all over the world including America

Glossary

neuroscientist: specialist in the study of the brain and the nervous system

Alzheimer's and Parkinson's diseases

In 1997 I set up my own company, Synaptica Ltd, so that I could carry on my research. I was interested in finding out about **Alzheimer's disease** and **Parkinson's disease**. Both are very serious brain diseases mainly affecting older people and making life very hard for them and for their families.

Some of the symptoms of Alzheimer's disease are:
- memory loss
- disorientation
- confusion
- depression
- worrying
- wandering

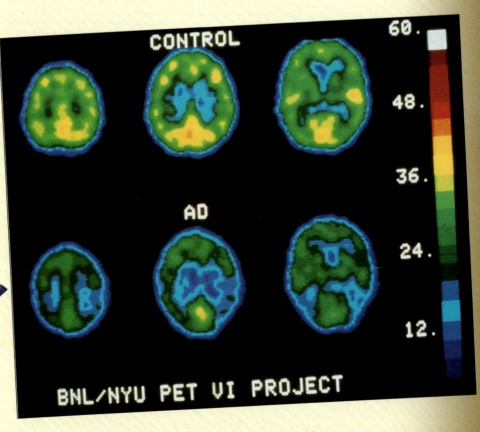

a scan of a normal brain

a scan of a brain affected by Alzheimer's disease

Some people with Parkinson's disease have difficulty in moving their arms and legs or swallowing food. For others their hands tremble so much that they cannot hold a cup.

The problem is in a very small part of the middle of the brain called the "black mass". For people with Parkinson's disease the brain cells of the black mass have died so that important chemicals cannot be made. It is not clear why or how this happens.

My dream is to find out more so that we can produce drugs which will stop those brain cells dying. It would be wonderful to be able to say to a person with Parkinson's disease, "Take this medicine and you will be able to live a more normal life."

We are not there yet but perhaps one day my dream will come true.

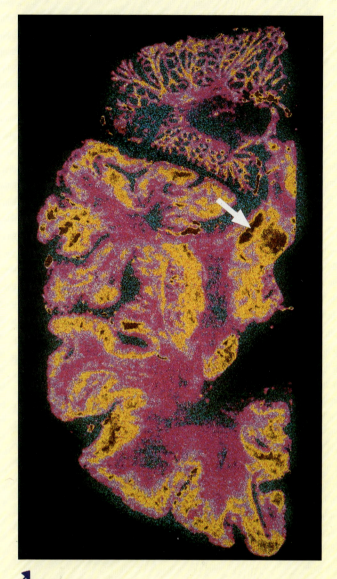

A scan of a brain affected by Parkinson's disease

Glossary

Alzheimer's disease: an illness causing damage to brain cells and to the sufferer's mental abilities

Parkinson's disease: an illness causing damage to brain cells and to the sufferer's physical abilities

What makes me do my work?

Sometimes people ask me why I work so hard and do so many different things in my life. That's not easy to answer but I do have clear ideas of what I want to achieve and why.

For example, I am not a medical doctor and I do not work in a hospital. But I do want my research to help people who are ill. I am lucky enough to have always been healthy and able to do my work. I think that I have the skills and knowledge to help people and that's what I want to do.

Nowadays both boys and girls do science in schools and go on to become doctors or dentists or scientists in industry. This has not always been the case. I want to show young people, especially girls, that they can succeed in scientific jobs if they work hard and make the most of school. My parents were not rich, but they helped me to do well. I hope that my story might inspire young people.

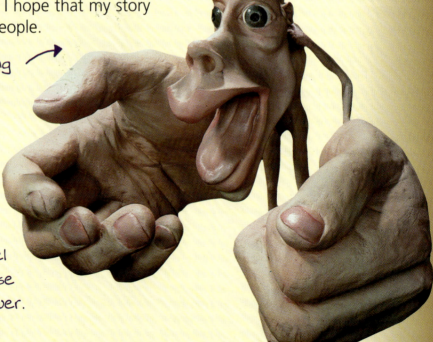

This strange looking object is called a homunculus model. Some parts of the body use more brain power than others. The sizes of the parts of this model show which ones use the most brain power.

I believe that everybody has the right to know about the latest scientific ideas because they affect our everyday lives. Just think how difficult it would be to deal with the problems of **AIDS**, **BSE** and **global warming**, for example, if we did not understand the science behind them.

Science can be fun!

GLOSSARY

AIDS (Acquired Immune Deficiency Syndrome): a very serious disease caused by the HIV virus, which attacks the body's immune system and weakens its defences against disease

BSE (Bovine Spongiform Encephalopathy): brain disease affecting cattle

global warming: climate change due to the build-up of "greenhouse gases" in the Earth's atmosphere

Who I really am

Although I am a serious scientist, people say that I do not look like one. I think that this is a compliment. I certainly do not always wear a white coat and spend my time doing dangerous experiments with chemicals in dusty laboratories! In fact I have a wardrobe full of colourful clothes. My favourite item is my red leather jacket. I like to wear stylish trousers and skirts with high-heeled shoes. I had my first lipstick when I was thirteen years old and I still prefer bright red shades.

I think my love of fashionable clothes comes from my mum. When I was a teenager she used to buy material from the local market and then sew the clothes that I had designed. They never cost much money but I always had lots of great things to wear and we had lots of fun making them.

My favourite jacket!

I think it helps sometimes that I look like a normal person rather than like a scientist because people seem to listen to what I have to say.

Presenting my TV show, 'Brain Story'

What I look and sound like is also important when I am in the newspapers or on television. In 2000 I made a series of six programmes about the brain and I know that many people watched. It was great to present serious science on television and to tell people all the things that I know about the brain. I think people understood what it was all about and that I was very enthusiastic.

Working at the Royal Institution

One of the ways in which I have been able to help more people understand the importance of science is to be the Director of the Royal Institution of Great Britain. This is a very important job and I am very proud to be the first woman ever to hold the post.

The Royal Institution is in London and it was founded in 1799. Many famous scientists, such as **Michael Faraday**, worked in the laboratories there and made important discoveries. It has a very good website (www.ri.ac.uk) so that everyone can find out more about what goes on.

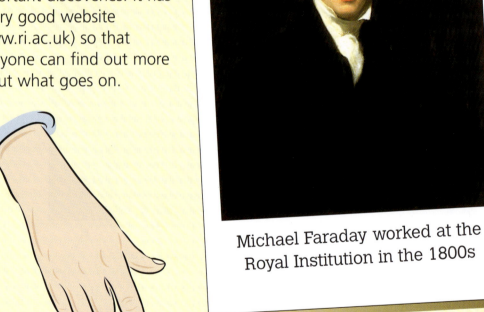

Michael Faraday worked at the Royal Institution in the 1800s

www.ri.ac.uk

All through the year we organise talks for adults about different topics in science. At Christmas time there are special lectures for young people which are also shown on television. They are always interesting, up to date with new ideas and above all they are exciting to watch. I hope that they inform young people about what is happening in the scientific world and motivate them to want to know more. That's what we are trying to do at the Royal Institution.

Now that I have become a member of the House of Lords I take part in the debates about science and issues that mainly affect women. When I was a young girl I always thought that it was only important people – people I would never meet – who made the big decisions about our lives. I can hardly believe that now I am one of those people! I want to do my job as a baroness properly.

Inside the House of Lords

Glossary

Michael Faraday: British chemist and physicist (1791–1867), who discovered the connection between electricity and magnetism

A typical day in Oxford

I still visit my company Synaptica and work at the University of Oxford two or three days each week. I live with my husband Peter in a lovely house with a swimming pool in the countryside just outside Oxford. We also have a small flat in the city close to my work.

I get up early and drive to the office and laboratories by 7 am. My secretary arrives at 8 am and we spend time reading the e-mails, taking phone messages, opening the post and talking about the plans for the day.

This is the office where I work, and this is Vivienne, my secretary.

Afterwards I meet the men and women who do the brain research work in the laboratory and they tell me about the progress they are making. I have a sandwich for lunch at work.

In the afternoons I often go back to my flat so that I can catch up on reading or do some writing for a new book or for a lecture that I have to give. I like the evenings very much because I can have a drink and meal in college with old Oxford friends. But we always get back home in good time so that we can have an early night and get ready for another busy day tomorrow.

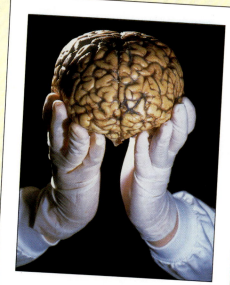

My work in the laboratory

Oxford is sometimes called, 'the city of dreaming spires' due to its many churches.

A typical week in my life

The Royal Institution in London was founded in 1799. This painting of it is from 1838.

When I am in London, life is very busy but also very varied. I spend two or three days working at the Royal Institution. It's a lovely old building but one of my aims is to modernise it. I want to make it open and friendly so that more people can come in and learn about science.

I have lunch with lots of people who want to help raise money for the Royal Institution.

Almost every week I fly to somewhere in Great Britain to give lectures, but I usually have to be back in London for public meetings and for special dinners in the evenings. Sometimes I go to schools to present prizes or to open new buildings.

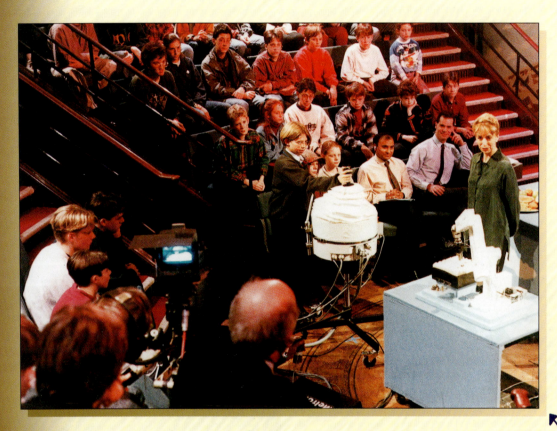

Me giving the Royal Institution Christmas lecture

Once or twice every month I go abroad either to speak at conferences about the brain or to raise funds for the Royal Institution. I have always been excited about flying and I still enjoy the thrills of taking off and landing somewhere different. I will be spending more time in London now that I have a seat in the House of Lords. It is all very new but I am looking forward to the challenge!

What have we learned about the brain?

It is very intriguing to look back on my work and see what has happened in the last twenty years or so. What do we know now about the brain that we did not know then?

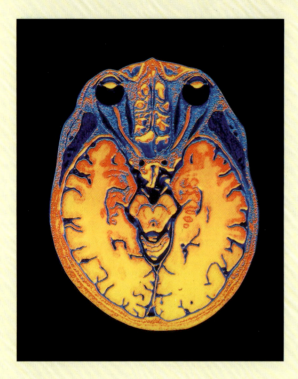

Neuroscience was unheard of in the past but now it is beginning to be a subject that students can take in schools when they do their A levels. That shows just how important the work on the brain is becoming.

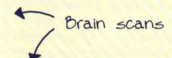

Brain scans

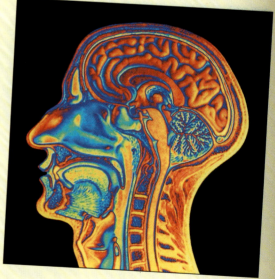

Doctors are now able to take pictures of the brain – brain scans – which show what is happening in different areas of the brain and if there are parts which are not working properly. Some of these pictures are very beautiful indeed and show just how wonderful and intricate the brain is.

I think that one of the most important things we have learned is the effect that drugs have on the brain. Of course in medicine some drugs are essential to keep people healthy, free from pain and in some cases to keep them alive.

But there are many other drugs which people take for pleasure – to give them a good feeling. I know from my research on the brain that this is very dangerous indeed. Drugs can actually change and damage parts of the brain and can lead to serious illness.

There are many things that you can do to keep the brain fit and to make you feel better:

As far as the brain goes you either use it or lose it!

- Make sure that the brain gets lots of oxygen – take deep breaths and get plenty of sleep and exercise.
- Keep the brain alert with different activities – try listening to new music or visit a new place.
- Make the brain work hard with games, puzzles and debates – anything that makes you think.
- Keep the brain active – stay open to new ideas and question how things are done.

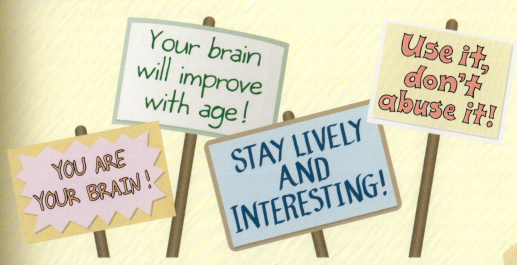

What might we learn in the future?

Life for me has changed so much from being a little girl in a London primary school to being a world expert on the brain and a member of the House of Lords. I have never been ambitious. But I have always taken the opportunities that have come my way and tried to enjoy what I am doing at the time. I guess I will carry on doing just that.

What about brain science? There is so much more to be found out – I think we have only just begun. I think that the next step will be to work out how the brain makes you the person you are. For example:

What makes you an easy-going person?

What makes you someone who loses his or her temper easily?

What makes you decide to do some things and not others?

What makes you work things out in a particular way which is different from the way your friend thinks?

This is more than an understanding of how the brain works. This is about your **mind** and what makes you the special person you are.

Glossary

mind: the unique mix of thoughts, feelings, imagination, memory and will that make up an individual's personality

I predict that there will be a new science which will have a new name – **neurotechnology**. Once scientists know more about the mind and how it works they may be able to change the chemicals and links in the brain which determine the mind. In fact this would change the person altogether. Doctors could use this technology to good effect and help people with certain mental illnesses to live healthier lives. But there could also be dangers if scientists misused their knowledge. That's true for all scientific discoveries. If the public do not understand what is happening in science they cannot have a say in how the scientific information should be used.

Now you can see why I believe it is so important for young people to study and enjoy science in schools. Only then will the next generation understand what is possible in our world and be able to influence what will happen.

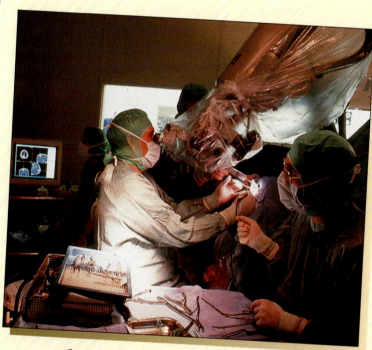

The future – computer based surgery support system

Glossary

neurotechnology: a new science dealing with connections in the brain and how these can be altered

Index

Alzheimer's disease 16–17

behaviour 11
books 5, 7, 15
brain 12–13, 28–30
    diseases 14, 16–17
    healthy 29

cerebellum 12
cerebrum 12
chemicals 14, 31
childhood 6–7
company 16, 24
conferences 27
control 12–13
cortex 13

disease 14, 16–17, 19
doctors 28, 31
drugs 29

exams 8–9

family 6–7, 9
fitness 29
friends 5–6
future 30–31

health 29
House of Lords 23

jobs 15, 18

laboratories 14–15, 22, 25
lectures 23, 27
London 26–27

medulla 13
meetings 27
messages 13
mind 30

neuroscience 14, 28
neurotechnology 30

Oxford University 9–11, 15, 24

parents 6–7
Parkinson's disease 16–17
psychology 9, 11

research 14–15, 18, 25
Royal Institution 22–23, 26

scans 28
school 2–3, 8–9, 18
science 8, 18–19, 23
scientists 18, 22, 31

teenage years 8–9, 20
television programmes 21, 23
thinking 11, 30
timeline 2–5

university 9–11, 15, 24

working day 24–25